D1470502

Open
His Gift

Dana Taggart

CSM Publishing

Open His Gift

Copyright© 2003 by Dana Taggart

First Printing	2003
Second Printing	2006
Third Printing	2009
Fourth Printing	2012
Fifth Printing	2015

All rights reserved. No part of this book may be reproduced in any form or by any electronic or mechanical means including information storage and retrieval systems without permission in writing from the copyright holder, except by a reviewer, who may quote brief passages in review.

ISBN: 0-9741858-0-9

www.openhisgift.com

CSM Publishing
P.O. Box 2656 MCPO
1266 Makati City, Philippines
E-mail: direct@csm-publishing.com

Dedicated
to
Judy Moore Kifer,
who
took the time
to
offer me His Gift

A Special Thank You

To my heavenly Father who has faithfully taught me His word. To my wonderful husband, George, who has always made it possible for me to be involved in activities for the kingdom, and to my precious dad, Richard Noble Conolly, who has encouraged and supported this endeavor from the beginning. To Sue Karcher, Ann Calhoun and Linda Beauchamp for their invaluable help in getting this off the ground.

Contents

Introduction

Still burning in my heart are the words used by one who helped me open His gift so many years ago. This single encounter with truth has made a lasting difference in my life. Although it cannot be purchased, when found, one would give everything to possess it. His gift lies within your reach. Do not miss it.

PART I

The Gift

There is a gift that makes all things new. If this gift is opened, life will never be the same, for the human heart involved has jumped the track on which this world races. Stepping out of mainstream, one is surprised to find former cherished pursuits abandoned along the way. They cannot compare with what is gained and the reality of what before was unseen.

What will transpire in your life cannot be described for this experience is unique for every individual. God has designed DNA and fingerprints for you alone, and His interaction with you regarding this gift will be equally personal. It is something only He can give.

God's gift is not at all another band-aid for what ails mankind and has little to do with one's circumstances. Countless situations, involving heartache and trial, may or may not change, but the gift God offers brings resilient hope to the heart and a security which cannot come from this world. Steadfast peace and anticipation of the future will prevail throughout the inevitable storms of life.

A Closer Look

For a closer look at the gift God has for man, we must turn to an ageless literary miracle, the Bible. People throughout history have died to keep this book in their possession, and centuries of critics have failed to remove it from the best-seller list. One might marvel that a book, promoting unconditional love and servanthood, is outlawed by entire cultures. It is outlawed because it transforms lives. The Bible has a power of its own. Brilliant skeptics, through the years, setting out to disprove its content end up on their knees in awe of the treasure they find. They uncover the gift.

The overriding theme of the Bible from beginning to end is the gift God has for man. That in itself is a miracle, for it is humanly impossible that a single volume, composed of over sixty individual books, would produce a unified system of information when written over a period of more than 1600 years by more than forty different men. Speaking different languages, living in different eras, and representing every walk of life from fisherman and shepherd to physician and king, not one of these men knew their writing would become part of a combined work. Yet all sixty-six books fit together perfectly with one continuing harmonious theme. Only God could orchestrate such a work.

Predictive Prophecy

Inspired by One who operates outside of our time domain, the Bible reveals history before it takes place. Men, moved by God, penned words we are told God watches over to perform. Almost one-fourth of Scripture is prophetic. Accurate, predictive prophecy sets this book apart from all others in the world.

Specific prophecies regarding individuals, cities, nations, and empires, which stand in opposition to the natural expectation of man, have come to pass exactly as Scripture has foretold. Archaeology, scholarship, and secular history contain irrefutable evidence of their fulfillment, which in most instances occurred centuries after the death of the prophet who wrote. They are coming to pass today.

Amazing Prophecies

No one can read prophecies such as those concerning the city of Tyre in the book of Ezekiel and then read the fulfillment recorded by secular historians without being awed by God's word. These prophecies (*Ezekiel 26*), given when Tyre was an impregnable fortress on the Mediterranean Sea, foretold the total destruction of Tyre; its rubble and logs would be placed in the water, and it would be swept clean of even the dust until it was but flat rock and a place to dry fishing nets. Every detail has come to pass beginning with the invasion of Babylonian armies and completed more than 200 years later when the troops of Alexander the Great used the thousands of tons of rubble lying in Tyre and placed it in the water to build a causeway in order to defeat New Tyre which had been built out on an island off the coast. Today, the site of ancient Tyre is flat rock where people dry fishing nets.

Reading the book of 1 Kings, people are amazed to realize God spoke of King Josiah by name over 250 years before Josiah was born (*1 Kings 13:2*). Likewise, in the book of Isaiah, God called Cyrus of Persia by name 150 years before Cyrus was born and told exactly how Cyrus as king would enter and defeat the invincible city of Babylon (*Isaiah 45*). Cyrus was born, became king, and defeated the Babylonians, just as God had said he would, without knowing of these prophecies.

Future World Empires Called By Name

The book of Daniel is a book one could spend a lifetime of study in, as it contains incredible visions and prophecies regarding all future world empires. Medo-Persia and Greece were so designated by name (*Daniel 8*) long before they were in existence as world powers. Greece was but a group of insignificant tribes not yet on the map.

Scholars, at times, have tried to explain away prophecy by attributing much later dates to certain books of the Bible, such as Daniel, but discoveries of ancient scrolls and scientific dating techniques have only served to substantiate the fact that Daniel's writings, as well as those of the other prophets, were inspired by God, who is not bound by time or space. He knows the beginning to the end and has chosen to reveal history to those who care to know.

Time Is Moving According To His Schedule

Prophecy continues to be fulfilled today as history unfolds. Nothing fosters greater security within the heart of man than to watch God's word come to pass exactly as He has said it would. Time is moving according to His schedule, approaching a day when all mankind will know there is a sovereign Creator of the universe who is personally involved with His creation.

A Scarlet Thread

Although most people today are aware of the Bible and may own multiple copies, a vast majority have no idea what its pages contain. Rare are those who unravel the scarlet thread which runs from one end of Scripture to the other, leading one to His gift. The book you hold is designed to reveal this scarlet thread, woven throughout Scripture, that seeking hearts might grasp what God desires to bestow.

A Glimpse Of His Gift

A portion of a verse in the book of Romans reveals a glimpse of the gift God has for man, stating:

> *the free **gift** of God is **eternal life** ...*
> *Romans 6:23*

According to this verse, anyone who receives God's gift will live forever in the hereafter. Yet Scripture reveals *all* of humanity will live forever in one destination or another, and it is very clear that not all people receive this gift. Therefore, there has to be something, besides living forever in the hereafter, that is different about the *gift of eternal life* which God gives to an individual.

The Miracle Of God's Gift

A key, to what that difference is, is found in the book of John when the words of Christ are recorded as He prayed for those who would receive this gift. The gift of eternal life is disclosed as Jesus says:

> *And this is eternal life, that they might know Thee, the only true God, and your Son Jesus Christ.*
> *John 17:3*

Read that verse carefully. It says that eternal life will bring an individual to the place wherein he or she will actually know *"the only true God."* This *is* the miracle of God's gift. One may *know God.* Eternal life is to know and experience personally the Creator of the universe. A finite human being is put in contact with the infinite God, and it happens in the here and now. God's gift of eternal life begins in this life. It is received this side of the grave or not at all.

Entering into this relationship is a personal transaction between one individual and God. When this transaction occurs, the door into God's presence is opened, bringing the opportunity for life of a quality never before experienced. On our own we stand no chance of coming into His presence or knowing Him, but God has made a way.

Knowing God surpasses all other experiences in life. God, Himself, initiates our introduction, reaching out to us long before we know Him. God already knows us intimately, numbering each hair on our heads, and He challenges us to turn from our worldly pursuits and to seek after Him. God says that "knowing Him" is the only thing we can legitimately boast about in this life. Scripture tells us:

> *Thus says the Lord, Let not a wise man boast*
> *of his wisdom, and let not the mighty man*
> *boast of his might, let not a rich man boast*
> *of his riches; but let him who boasts boast of*
> *this, that he understands and knows Me.*
> *Jeremiah 9:23, 24a*

God would not make that declaration if it were not within the realm of possibility for us to experience, and He has indeed made it possible.

Until one knows the Creator, there is no real peace in life. There may be great diversion, fleeting fulfillment, much comfort and ease, even worldly acclaim, but underneath it all, within the heart of man, lie doubt and insecurity. The innermost self, by design, finds rest and true fulfillment only in relationship with Him. Man hungers for this until He knows God.

A Plan

Before the foundation of the earth was laid, God had a plan spanning eternity. The word *eternal* denotes not just forever future but also forever past. Not one of us has existed eternally, except in the heart of our Creator. If we are His, He has always known us. We are part of His eternal plan.

God knew when and where you would be born and He knew what you would look like. God has also known exactly how your heart would respond to Him and to the offer of His gift. Let's look at a panoramic view of why God chose this particular gift, how it came to be, and how one enters into this one vital love relationship in life.

God's Gift Costly, But Necessary

God's gift had to be. To understand why something so costly was necessary, one must go back to creation. You will enjoy this story for you are personally involved from the beginning to the end.

His Plan

God is One God, yet He is three different persons. Difficult to grasp is the fact that God the Father, Jesus Christ the Son, and the Holy Spirit are *three-in-one*. They are coequal Beings who have worked together in indivisible unison from eternity past. Following their individual roles throughout Scripture, we discover that from the beginning of time:

> *God the Father has conceived a plan,*
> *Jesus the Son has carried out the plan,*
> *And the Holy Spirit reveals the plan to man.*

All three have been involved from the beginning of creation. Like clockwork through the ages, God's plan has come to pass and is still in process today.

God Had No Beginning

God is eternal. He has always been. Everything else in our universe has been brought into existence according to

His plan through creative acts carried out by the Son. Scripture, speaking of Jesus Christ, tells us:

> *For by Him all things were created, both in the heavens and on earth, visible and invisible, whether thrones or dominions or rulers or authorities—all things have been created by Him and for Him.*
>
> *Colossians 1:16*

According to Scripture, Jesus Christ created everything that has ever been created, and all that has been created is for Him.

Scholars debate theories concerning creation; a debate that will continue until all things are known. There are answers in this life which remain with God alone, who operates outside of time, space, and gravity as we know it, but God has clearly revealed Himself as Creator of all that is.

One Tiny Planet

Somewhere, in the midst of a vast solar system in a galaxy known today as the Milky Way, God placed a pinpoint of a planet, Earth. Smaller than the smallest star, Earth would seem destined to relative obscurity in the overall scheme of creation, yet the Bible attaches an astounding importance to planet Earth.

Scripture reveals God created the entire universe expressly for this one tiny planet, placing bodies in the heavens to give light and provide signs and seasons for Earth. Genesis relates:

> *Then God said, Let there be lights in the expanse of the heavens to separate the day*

from the night, and let them be for signs,
and for seasons, and for days and years; and
let them be for lights in the expanse of the
heavens to give light on earth and it was so.
Genesis 1:14, 15

For centuries man has navigated by the stars and been illuminated and warmed by the sun. The solar system has provided the light necessary for vegetation to grow. Our solar system is also the perfect timepiece. Every clock in existence can run down, but God's clock does not miss a second. God incomprehensibly finely tuned this universe and balanced it to a mathematically infinitesimal degree to support life on this planet. He created this perfect system for Earth.

Life

Plant life, birds of the air, marine and animal life were brought forth on this small terrestrial ball. Unlike the stars, these new life forms had the ability to grow and reproduce their kind.

In the beginning, nature was a symphony of beauty, harmony, and balance. Destructive weather did not exist. Weeds did not choke out foliage. Fleas did not bite dogs, and wolves did not eat lambs. Nothing was carnivorous. With neither predator nor prey, an abundance of fruit, vegetables, and grain supported all life. Earth, arrayed as God intended, was a paradise of beauty and peace difficult to imagine today.

Why?

Why would God go to such lengths? Why did God single out one small planet in the midst of a vast universe?

What would He do with this paradise He had created? What was His purpose?

From the beginning, God the Father had one objective. He was after one thing, and Earth, formed in perfection, was primed to receive the climax of all that had come from His hand.

An Eternal Family

God's passion and desire was for an eternal family. With His father's heart, God fashioned the first human being, the highest form of physical life. Created in God's own image, a man and a woman were brought forth as adults and placed in a garden.

The Biblical statement that one man and one woman began the human race has long been called into question, but today, genetic research on female genes from races around the world has proven that every person alive on earth shares one common female ancestor. Modern science, like Scripture, refers to this original female as "Eve" meaning *life-producer.* Man too is traced back to one original male, "Adam," a word which carries the connotation of *mankind.*

The Bible And Science

The Bible is not an exhaustive text on science, but when touching this realm, it is without error and may reveal truth hundreds or thousands of years before man gains that knowledge experientially. That currents exist in the sea (*Psalms 8:8*) and that things visible are composed of things invisible (*Hebrews 11:3*) were indicated in Scripture long before these facts were established by man.

The Gift Of Creativity

The pinnacles of creation, Adam and Eve, were gifted with extraordinary minds and the ability to create. God is the infinite Creator, creating out of nothing. Man, made in God's image, is able to create out of the mind, abilities, and materials given to him by God.

In all the world, man alone is innovative and creative. Other creatures are locked into set patterns of innate behavior, communication, and instinct, within which they build, bond, and forage for sustenance. They do not operate outside of God-given instinct. Each species has built the same nest, den, or lair in basically the same style and materials for thousands of years, rarely varying in design. They have no innovative architects. The ability to write, invent, design, and compose is unique to a human being who mirrors the image of his Creator.

One Critical Difference

God placed Adam and Eve in dominion over all that He had made, telling them to be fruitful and to multiply and to subdue the earth. Together they became something that apart they could never be. Adam and Eve possessed physical and emotional needs similar to our own. Observing them, one might think that they were identical to all humanity which followed, but they were not. There was something about Adam and Eve that was unique. From the beginning, one critical difference set them apart forever from all other humans who would follow.

Perfection

Unlike the rest of mankind, God created both Adam and Eve in total perfection. They were *perfect*; they were *sinless.* Brought forth in God's image, Adam and Eve had no sin, nor did they possess a nature with the inclination to sin, which causes alienation or separation from God, who is perfect.

The root word for "sin," an archery term, means *missing the mark.* The root word for "perfect" means *hitting the mark.* By design, Adam and Eve were created hitting the mark. They measured up to God's standard of perfection, a condition necessary in order for Adam and Eve to have a relationship with their Creator. God is perfect holiness, and by His own nature has no relationship with that which is imperfect.

They Knew God

In their perfection, Adam and Eve readily enjoyed God's ultimate gift. They *knew God.* They were able to communicate intimately with their Creator. Knowing Him was the source of joy, fulfillment, and purpose in their lives.

A Free Will

Although Adam and Eve were created without a sinful nature, God made both of them free moral agents. They had absolute freedom to make decisions outside of the will of their Creator if they chose to do so. Communicating with God and fulfilling the purpose for which one is intended will always involve obedience to the revealed will of God. Adam and Eve would individually decide whether to live under God's authority or their own.

God Did Not Create Puppets

God created Adam and Eve in His own image to share an intimate, love relationship with Him. Above all, God desired their love and obedience, but He did not want it at the expense of their own free will. In order for a true love relationship to exist, man has to have the freedom to reject God.

God could have designed this first couple and all of their descendants to love, worship, and obey Him automatically, but He chose not to do that. God does not desire a planet of puppets. He is the Lover of every person in this universe and has loved us first. He reveals Himself to every individual, drawing each one to return His love, but people may choose to go their own way. Choosing to respond to God in love, is a gift of grace from God.

God is still at work in hearts today. God reaches out to each one of us, and we, like Adam and Eve, make choices every day. The Bible reveals that the decisions made in this life carve out our future for all eternity.

The Test

God knew difficult choices lay ahead for Adam and Eve when He gave them free will. Freedom of choice is meaningless if there is only one path to take. God was aware another with evil intent would also desire the allegiance of Adam and Eve. To protect them, Adam was given a grave warning.

God singled out the fruit of one tree in the garden which was not to be eaten. Everything necessary to sustain Adam and Eve physically, emotionally, and spiritually had been provided for in abundance. Their body's needs were to be satisfied with every fruit and grain of the land, but God told Adam that the day he ate from the "tree of the knowledge of good and evil" he would die. Only after bringing Adam to a full understanding of this one boundary in life did God allow man's loyalty to be tested.

The Adversary

Temptation came. Satan, whom the Bible refers to as "the prince and power of this atmosphere," was in the garden. The Tempter, whose name "Satan" means *adversary*, is also known as the Devil in Scripture. Long ridiculed, the thought of a personal devil is no longer dismissed as police forces are forced to attend seminars to equip them to deal with the bizarre atrocities associated with Satan worship. His existence is taught in seven books of the Old Testament and by every New Testament author. Throughout history people have worshiped and served Satan.

A Fallen Angel

There are questions as to Satan's origin and realm, but he is revealed in Scripture as a fallen angel. Angels are spiritual beings created by God to serve Him. Normally not seen by the human eye, angels, at times, manifest themselves on earth in physical form and are greater in intellect, strength, and speed than men. Holding various ranks of ministry and power, angels, like human beings, have freedom to choose God's will or their own.

Extraordinarily powerful and possessing great beauty, charisma, and intellect, Satan, according to Scripture, at one time held one of the highest positions of honor and responsibility in Heaven, but his personal ambition became rebellion (*Isaiah 14:12-14*). Desiring his own throne elevated and himself exalted, Satan and other angels who chose to follow him were cast out of Heaven, beginning a war which continues to this day.

Since that time, angels have existed in both their original and fallen states. God has His orders of angels and Satan has his. Scripture reveals that God's angelic host carry out divine directives, which include rendering aid and protection to God's children on earth (*Hebrews 1:14*). Satan's angels, known as demons, oppose all that God stands for and work against those who carry out God's work on earth.

God rules over Satan and the demonic realm as He does over all creation, but Scripture indicates He has allowed Satan a government of his own and certain powers for a period of time. The Bible reveals that at a future appointed time, God will decisively deal with Satan, his angels, and all people who have not established a relationship with God during their life on earth.

Angels Cannot Reproduce

Although it may appear that Satanic forces are increasing in number and strength at times, angels do not possess the ability to reproduce. They are not increasing in number but, unlike man, they are not subject to death. The same angels have been around throughout the ages. As a culture or individual turns away from God's revealed will, demonic powers have more freedom to promote evil throughout a society or an individual life.

Satanic deception comes in many different forms. Unwary people may be taken in by a psychic, fortune teller or taro card reader who is able to reveal personal information concerning them that no one could possibly know. They are unaware that those who have entered into deeper levels of witchcraft and the occult may possess supernatural powers and knowledge. The Bible never says there is not reality in the occult. It just says not to have anything to do with it.

Scripture warns about Satan and his angels and their capacity for evil. We are told in the book of Ephesians:

> *Put on the full armor of God that you may*
> *be able to stand firm against the schemes of*
> *the devil. For our struggle is not against flesh*

> *and blood, but against the rulers, against the*
> *powers, against the world forces of this*
> *darkness, against the spiritual forces of*
> *wickedness in the heavenly places.*
>
> *Ephesians 6:11-12*

An Angel Of Light

Satan's initial approach was to the woman in the garden. Neither sinister nor evil in appearance, Satan appeared in a form personally enticing to Eve. He does not come to an individual as an evil looking character as he is often depicted. According to Scripture, Satan appears as *an angel of light* (*2 Corinthians 11:14*). Appealing to natural desires in an area he has observed an individual to be vulnerable, he comes in whatever form it takes to achieve the results he desires. Working through people who belong to him, Satan brings difficulties into the lives of those who serve God.

Eve was his first victim. Taking her eyes off of all she had been given by God, Satan had Eve focus on the one thing that was forbidden. He refuted God's warning about death and caused Eve to doubt God's goodness. Offering her the forbidden fruit, Satan deceived Eve and she ate.

Adam followed in her footsteps, but he did so in the full knowledge that he was stepping over the one boundary God had placed on his life. Adam took what God had asked him not to eat. Through willful disobedience, he removed himself from God's authority, and when he did, sin entered into the nature of man. As Adam took this step outside of God's revealed will, he had no idea of the monumental repercussions which would follow. Life as Adam and Eve had known it would never be the same.

Spiritual Death

God had told Adam he would die if he ate from that tree. Did he die? Physically, no. His physical body did not miss a heartbeat. But just as God had warned, Adam died. Far more devastating than physical death is spiritual death. Adam experienced spiritual death the moment he took that first bite. His spirit, that part of him which had enjoyed communion with his Creator, died that instant.

Body, Soul, And Spirit

Man is body, soul, and spirit. The body is our physical being with which we touch, taste, hear, see, and smell. The soul is made up of our intellect, will, and emotion. Most people live out their lives thinking that is all there is, but there is also a spirit within every individual which is eternal. It is our spirit that possesses the potential to move out of the physical realm and communicate with our Creator. God is spirit and He relates *spirit to spirit*, God's spirit to a man's spirit. Scripture tells us,

> *God is spirit, and those who worship Him*
> *must worship in spirit and truth.*
> *John 4:24*

Suffering spiritual death, Adam and Eve were suddenly cut off from God. True death, according to Scripture, is spiritual death which results in separation from and a life void of communication with God.

Intimacy With God No Longer Possible

Spiritually dead, Adam and Eve no longer experienced the peace, security, and joy of a relationship with the One who formed them. Intimacy with their Creator was no longer possible. God had created them for His own eternal enjoyment, but, true to His nature of perfect holiness, His fellowship was no longer experienced by Adam and Eve, who had become imperfect. Having partaken from the "tree of the knowledge of good and evil," Adam and Eve, for the first time, experienced internal tension for they now possessed the knowledge of both good and evil. Henceforth they would desire to do good, but they would be drawn toward evil. A daily battle began within the minds of Adam and Eve.

Death Passed On To Offspring

The aftereffects of Adam's disobedience are staggering. His spiritual death would affect not just Adam but also his children and grandchildren. All future generations would be born spiritually dead. The nature of man is passed from generation to generation. Since all of us descended from Adam, a sinful nature has been passed on to all mankind. As infants, we arrive in this world separated from God.

Adam and Eve's first two children, Cain and Abel, were possibly adorable toddlers, but when Eve held Cain, her firstborn, she was holding a murderer. Jealousy would drive Cain to kill his brother Abel as sin began its devastating toll on creation.

Two Different Seeds

Everyone from Cain and Abel on has been born spiritually dead, and from that time forward, two different seeds have grown up among men. In every generation there exists a godly seed, evident when an individual, through God's grace, comes to see himself as he truly is, a sinner separated from his Creator. He realizes he is in need of help beyond himself, and he responds to God.

The other seed is made up of those who may outwardly appear to be upstanding, excellent in character, and even religious, but inwardly they have never had a personal encounter with their living Creator. Spiritually dead, they pass through life with an independent spirit relying on self and the philosophies of man. Each one of us falls into one of these two categories today, either spiritually alive to God or spiritually dead.

Cain and Abel were the first to inherit a sinful nature from their father, Adam. Both arrived with a built-in problem, separation from God. Of Adam and Eve's first two offspring, Abel grew and developed an attitude of love and obedience to God, while Cain harbored rebellion in his heart. Cain would have his own way.

As a result of the fall of Adam, each one of us comes into this world with the same problem Cain and Abel had. We arrive alienated from our Creator, wanting our own way. Perhaps it begins with us screaming to have a diaper changed and to be fed now! Inherited sin prohibits us from knowing God and experiencing the life that He designed us to have. We can trace this problem back to the garden. Scripture states:

> *... through one man sin entered into the world and death (separation from God) through sin, and so death spread to all men, because all sinned ...*
>
> *Romans 5:12*

Earth Cursed

The drastic downward spiral of life for Adam and Eve would continue. A curse came forth on Earth as man chose to align himself with Satan's desires rather than God's. Adam would now work by the sweat of his brow, and woman would bring forth children in pain. The process of aging began which inevitably leads to physical degeneration and death. Thorns and thistles sprang forth along with predators of every kind. Evil sowed fear, hatred, and jealousy, disrupting the harmony and peace on earth God intended man to have.

Paradise was lost. But God was not surprised by Adam's decision, for even then God had a plan whereby He would redeem His broken universe and mankind, whom He loved.

The Scarlet Thread

Having eaten from the forbidden tree, Adam and Eve fled into the garden. Suddenly self-conscious, they covered themselves with fig leaves. Those fig leaves, representing fallen man's effort to make himself presentable in God's eyes, marked the beginning of religion.

Religion is man's attempt to work his way into God's favor. We still try today. Subconsciously striving for His approval, we may go to church, give money to charitable causes, and attempt to live a wholesome life, trying not to cheat at school, on a spouse, or income tax. Religion can be tradition, ritual, ceremony, being baptized, taking communion, or any other religious exercise. But God is interested in relationship, not religion. God looks at any attempt to come to Him on human terms in the same way He looked at those fig leaves on Adam and Eve.

Our Most Noble Efforts Are Insufficient

Fig leaves and works will never do. It is not that these efforts are worthless. Far from it, much good can come from them. But if we are counting on any of these things to justify coming into God's presence and making it into heaven one day, we are doomed to failure. Our most noble efforts are insufficient because in God's economy a price has to be paid to restore the relationship between a Holy God and sinful man.

God is not just perfect holiness, He is perfect justice. His justice requires that a price be paid in order to take care of the sin causing separation between Himself and man. A plan that God foreknew would be necessary was now put into motion to pay the price to reconcile man to Himself.

The Price

To implement this plan, God did something very strange. Killing an animal, God shed the first blood that had ever been shed on Earth. He then covered Adam and Eve with the skin of that animal, replacing their fig leaves with His own provision.

Blood was the price to be paid. This began a pattern laid out by God which was to continue for thousands of years, whereby an imperfect, sinful man could once again come into the presence of a Holy God through the shedding of blood. Throughout Scripture, we can trace this one consistent requirement of God.

The Scarlet Thread

Blood is the scarlet thread that runs from one end of the Bible to the other, blood offered for sin on God's altar. From the fall of mankind, God had an answer for man's dilemma so that we would not remain separated from our Creator.

God made it possible for everyone to meet His requirement of a blood offering. If a person could not afford a lamb, a goat, or a calf, one could obtain a pigeon or a turtledove, both of which were free and plentiful. But blood had to be shed. It was the legal transaction necessary in order to come into God's presence. All were to approach God's presence through blood. This requirement still holds true today. We are told in the 17th chapter of the book of Leviticus:

> *For the life of the flesh is in the blood, and I have given it to you on the altar to make atonement for your souls; for it is the blood by reason of the life that makes atonement.*
> *Leviticus 17:11*

Blood is the life of all flesh. If blood ceases to reach cells of the tissue of any flesh, that flesh dies. No man is pronounced dead until his blood circulation has ceased. God says that it is blood, the mysterious life giving force of living flesh, that makes atonement for sin.

Atonement means to make amends or give satisfaction for wrongdoing. From Genesis to Revelation, we have this message of atoning blood, blood on God's altar satisfies and makes amends for the sin of mankind.

We may experience revulsion at the thought of God demanding blood sacrifice, but this demand reveals the perfect balance in God's character. He is a God of love, but He has wrath for sin. He does not ignore sin. His very nature demands He do something about it.

It is interesting that today it is worshipers of Satan who sacrifice blood on Satan's altar. Revealed in the Bible as the great counterfeiter, Satan mimics God even in the area of blood sacrifice. He perverts that which God means for good.

Shedding the blood of an animal as an offering for sin made it possible to have communion with God, but the blood of an animal only "covered" sin. It was a stopgap, temporary solution which had to be repeated time and time again.

A Mystery

This was not always to be. Even in the garden of Eden God revealed a mystery which brought hope to man. One day God Himself would provide a sacrifice which would not just "cover" sin but would take away the penalty of sin completely and forever. Every blood sacrifice of an animal or bird pointed to a greater sacrifice yet to come. God would ultimately send One whose heel, according to Scripture, would be bruised by Satan but One who would deliver a death blow to the head of Satan. This Savior, the Messiah, would be called "Immanuel," meaning God with us.

Above all else, God wanted mankind to recognize the Messiah when He came. Therefore, God left substantial clues. Over hundreds of years throughout the Old Testament, God inspired men to record very specific prophecies concerning the coming Messiah. Woven into Scripture was a wide spectrum of detailed things to look for in this One who was to be the instrument of restoration.

Specific Prophecies Concerning The Messiah

Foretold, hundreds of years before His birth, was the fact that His mother would be a Jewish virgin, and He would be born in Bethlehem. He would be of the tribe of Judah and of the seed of Abraham. King David would be His ancestor. He would be called out of Egypt and known as a Nazarene. The lame, blind, deaf, and dumb would be healed by His touch. He would minister to the Gentiles. He would raise the dead. He would be revealed as the Messiah 483 years after a decree was issued to rebuild Jerusalem following the Babylonian captivity. At one point, He would ride into Jerusalem on a donkey. He would be betrayed by a friend for thirty pieces of silver, and that money would ultimately be used to purchase a potter's field. He would be beaten, spat upon, and disfigured through cruelty. Tormenters would pluck out His beard. He would be forsaken by His disciples. He would be rendered up as a guilt offering. He was to give His body as a ransom for others. The gruesome details of His death by crucifixion were described in detail hundreds of years before this form of death was ever devised. His hands and feet would be pierced. Not one of His bones would be broken. Men would gamble for His clothing as He died. Death would occur with common criminals, yet He was to be buried in a rich man's grave. He would be raised from the dead. He would ascend into heaven.

These and many other details of His life were revealed in Scripture. More than three hundred prophecies were recorded by men prompted by the Spirit of God generations before this Savior was born. Today, the majority of prophecies concerning the Messiah have been fulfilled and have come to pass exactly as foretold. Others have yet to be fulfilled.

Mathematically Impossible

Statistics show it is mathematically impossible for one-tenth of these specific prophecies concerning a single individual to be fulfilled apart from a miracle. During the centuries, many false Messiahs have claimed to be the One to whom God pointed, yet each has failed to fulfill even three or four of the specific prophecies of the Old

Testament, and not one has held up the prophecies to substantiate his claim. Any one or two of the prophecies by themselves would be weak evidence, but the number fulfilled in the life of the One God was going to send would form a wall of irrefutable evidence beyond human explanation. God would bring this to pass.

The entire Old Testament was written to let man know that help was on the way. If we refine the entire message of the Old Testament down to one sentence, God is saying to us:

> *We have a problem. We are separated, but I am going to do something about it.*

The entire New Testament was written to let us know that help has arrived. The whole message of the New Testament is God proclaiming the good news:

> *I did it. I have done something about our separation.*

A Birth Unlike Any Other

The clock of history ticked along. Thousands of years passed, but at the appointed time, within the womb of a young Jewish virgin, a baby was conceived. The virgin's name was Mary and the child she carried, conceived by the Holy Spirit, was part of God's plan. He would become the Messiah of the world. Mary was honored as the human vessel chosen by God to carry this child, but the life of Mary was never imparted to her child. His life had come from the Holy Spirit.

Conceived By The Holy Spirit

Jesus Christ was that infant conceived unlike any other since time began. He could not be born in the normal birth process, for sin had been passed from generation to generation through man. Of necessity, this birth would produce a perfect child without a sinful nature in order to fulfill the role He was to play in history. Conceived by the Holy Spirit, not by fallen man, Jesus Christ would come forth from the womb with a sinless nature.

Jesus was the second Adam, a perfect being. Yet he was more. He was fully man and He was fully God. This time God sent not just someone like Adam, created in His image without a sinful nature, He sent Himself. In a birth that angels observed with wonder, God came to earth in the form of a baby born into a common family.

Jesus Christ was to grow and become in the flesh all that the Father is. Jesus was the personality, the emotion, the will, the intellect, the power, and the wisdom of God Himself. Man has asked through the years, "Why would God become a man?"

It was men and women of flesh that God wanted to reach when He chose to become a physical man. God desired that we know Him, know the requirements He places on our life, and experience the depth of love He has for the human race. God was getting ready to reveal, through His Son, the heart of the Father and the lengths to which He was willing to go to restore mankind to Himself.

Little Known Of His Childhood

Little is recorded of the childhood of Jesus Christ other than that as He grew, He increased in strength and wisdom and He found favor with God and man. Whether Jesus grew up knowing who He was or heard of His unusual birth from family and neighbors is not known, but Scripture reveals that as a child He astounded the religious scholars of that day with His grasp of the Scriptures.

Physically, mentally, and emotionally Jesus grew to experience the joy, excitement, disappointment, and pain, and temptation common to man in life. Tempted in all things man is, Jesus chose to live a sinless life in compliance with His Father's will. In the face of unimaginable temptation. He proved immovable. Throughout his life, Jesus Christ consistently died to the desires of His flesh. His dying to self would become the trademark of His ministry and the example He would hold up for others to imitate.

At the age of thirty, Jesus Christ began a public and private ministry reaching out to people from all walks of life. As if magnetized, Jesus attracted crowds wherever He went. People marveled at His teaching, recognizing truth and wisdom never before heard. He spoke with authority. His words were supernatural, going deep inside, either drawing and changing or deeply offending. Those who heard Jesus Christ did not yet realize God was in their midst.

Twelve Men

Out of these crowds came an inner circle of handpicked disciples who dropped fishing nets, closed accounting books, and abandoned occupations when Jesus said, "Follow me." Twelve men left family, friends, and livelihood to become personally involved in the ministry and miracles of Jesus Christ. Eleven of these twelve would eventually spearhead a movement that would change the course of world history.

The miracles Jesus Christ performed were not of this world. The blind saw, the deaf heard, the lame leapt, and leprosy disappeared. At a word from Jesus Christ, violent, naked, insane men became calm and of a sound mind. Demons recognized Him and left at His command. The wind and the waves were subject to Him.

Eventually His name became a household word as thousands came to observe His miracles and hear Him teach. Within the multitudes, however, was a group of men who watched Jesus Christ for a different reason.

Powerful, Corrupt Men

Considered Israel's most upstanding citizens, the Jewish religious leaders did not like what they saw. Witnessing the response of the crowds to Jesus Christ, these men became increasingly bitter and jealous. Prior to this time, they had provided spiritual guidance for the people of Israel, and they were indignant at accolades being given to a Jewish peasant carpenter.

Loaded Questions

Seeking to discredit Him in the eyes of His followers, these leaders began in earnest to try to trap Jesus Christ through loaded questions. But Jesus always had an answer that left them speechless, and they would ultimately leave in frustration.

Jesus Christ threatened their prestige and their pocketbooks. He openly called the outer courtyard of the temple, which these men controlled, a "den of thieves." Jesus overturned their moneychanging tables, where exorbitant rates were charged to travelers coming into Jerusalem for religious feast days. He openly exposed the false shepherds for what they were, and tempers flared when these powerful, corrupt men were humiliated.

Late in His ministry, when Jesus raised Lazarus from the dead, the hatred and fear of these opponents solidified into plans for His arrest and execution.

They Should Have Known

Above all others, these religious leaders should have recognized Jesus Christ as the Messiah. They knew the Old Testament Scriptures containing the Messianic prophecies better than anyone else. Their religion of works produced some of the most outwardly upright people who have ever lived, but inside they were closed and cold. Jesus reached out to these men on numerous occasions, but they refused to hear truth. The scribes and pharisees of Israel stand out in history as classic examples of *ritual and religion without relationship*.

These religious conspirators would go on to pay the disciple Judas Iscariot thirty pieces of silver to lead them to Jesus Christ. This fulfilled the prophecies that the Messiah would be betrayed by a friend and for that exact sum of money. The money would return to these leaders when Judas, overcome with guilt for betraying an innocent man, hurled the coins into the temple. Fulfilling yet another prophecy, the money Judas returned was used to purchase a worthless potter's field that would become a burial ground.

Illegal Procedures

The religious rulers of Israel broke their own rules. Hiring false witnesses, they held trials during illegal hours, in private homes, using illegal procedures in which they convicted Jesus Christ, the Son of God, of blasphemy. They then stood and watched as He was spat on, blindfolded, mocked, and beaten.

They Would Have Their Way

The elders of Israel did not stop there. Satisfied with nothing short of death, they delivered Jesus Christ to the Roman governor, Pontius Pilate, who alone in the city had the power to execute a death sentence. Scripture records that Pilate was aware these men had ulterior motives and that he attempted to dissuade them several times, but with support from a mob they incited, the hierarchy of Israel was able to exert political pressure on Pontius Pilate until their tactics prevailed. Ultimately, they had their way. Jesus Christ would be nailed to a cross.

The Cross

Designed to inflict as much pain as possible for as long as possible, Roman crucifixion stands as one of the cruelest forms of execution in the history of mankind. The first step in the crucifixion process was flogging with the infamous cat-of-nine-tails, leather strips embedded with bone and metal which tore out flesh as it passed across bare skin. Only forty lashes were given as more might cause premature death. The person administering the lashes habitually stopped at thirty-nine, in fear of going beyond the allowed forty which incurred a penalty of being whipped with those same nine tails.

Mockery And Ridicule

His back and rib cage laid open, Jesus was dressed in scarlet as a king. His fame preceded Him and the Roman soldiers took full advantage. Weaving a crown of thorns, they spit on Him and bowed before Him as they hailed Him "King of the Jews." Jesus Christ refused to respond, fulfilling Isaiah's prophecy that He would go as a lamb to the slaughter and not open His mouth.

At the appointed time, Jesus was led out of Jerusalem toward the crucifixion site. Forced to carry the crossbar from which He would hang, Jesus fell under its weight in His weakened condition and had to be relieved along the way.

Arriving at Golgotha hill, He was stripped of His clothing, stretched on the timber, and nailed to the wood with metal spikes. With pain raging through His body, Jesus Christ was lifted up as the crossbar dropped into place.

The Next Hours

All of history revolves around what transpired during the next hours. Men and women who watched the blood flow out of Jesus Christ on Calvary were unaware they were witnessing the single most important event ever to take place on earth since the dawn of creation. Total darkness fell upon the land at high noon, and later, an earthquake rocked the land, but the eerie darkness and quaking earth in no way reflected the magnitude of what was taking place. Callous, unknowing men were carrying out God's plan of the ages.

Jesus prayed for these men from the cross saying, *"Father, forgive them; for they do not know what they are doing."* Jesus saw them for who they were, victims of circumstance and their own human natures.

The Crisis Of The Ages

Jesus Christ was nailed to the cross a perfect man. In His perfection, He remained intimately connected to His Father as is evidenced by His prayers to God from the cross. But as the day wore on, the incredible happened. The silence of that dark afternoon was suddenly shattered. The crisis of the ages came as Jesus Christ gave an agonizing cry, *"My God, My God, why have You forsaken Me?"*

Why This Cry?

Why? Why would Jesus cry out like this to God the Father? Surely Jesus would not be abandoned by His Father in His hour of greatest need? Jesus had committed no wrong. He was carrying out the will of His Father, so why would God forsake His Son when He was in agony? We can never understand what happened on the cross until we answer this question.

The Impossible Happened

In a moment planned from the foundation of the earth, the impossible happened. Jesus Christ, as a man, *was abandoned* by God the Father. The Father and the Son were *separated*. This separation was inevitable, for in that moment, God the Father transferred the sin of the world to Jesus Christ His Son, who willingly accepted it.

My sin became His. Your past, present, and future sin became His. Every lie, every jealous thought, every word of gossip, murder, act of incest, rape, adultery, theft, injustice, and human failure was transferred to Jesus Christ. Jesus Christ, the man, was no longer perfect. At this moment, God, true to His holy and perfect nature, turned away from sin.

His Greatest Pain

Jesus had endured betrayal by a close friend, the cat-of-nine-tails, the spitting, the ridicule and insults, desertion by His disciples, and the nails of the cross without objection. But when the sin of the world became His, for the first time Christ, as a man, experienced a barrier between Himself and a Holy God. His oneness with His Father was broken, and He cried out in His greatest loss and unimaginable pain.

For thousands of years, according to God's law, a priest had ritually transferred the guilt of human sin to an innocent animal as its blood was shed, foreshadowing the time when a final sacrifice would be made. Now, God transferred all sin to an innocent, perfect man, His Son Jesus Christ. We are told:

> *He made Him who knew no sin to be sin on our behalf, that we might become the righteousness of God in Him.*
> *2 Corinthians 5:21*

As His sinless blood was shed on Calvary, Jesus became the scapegoat for all mankind on the cross. The book of Hebrews tells us:

> *By this will we have been sanctified through the offering of the body of Jesus Christ once for all. And every priest stands daily ministering and offering time after time the same sacrifices, which can never take away sins; but He, having offered one sacrifice for sins for all time, sat down at the right hand of God.*
> *Hebrews 10:10-12*

The Scarlet Thread

Every blood sacrifice God had required during previous generations pointed to this once-for-all sacrifice. We can follow the scarlet thread of blood sacrifice throughout Scripture. It leads directly to the cross and to the blood of Jesus Christ.

For centuries, lambs and goats had been used as sacrifices to cover sin temporarily, but the sacrifice of sinless blood from God Himself, who had become a kinsman of Adam, had the power to remove forever the penalty of sin and redeem mankind. Scripture tells us:

> *... you were not redeemed with perishable things like silver or gold ... but with precious blood, as of a lamb unblemished and spotless, the blood of Christ.*
>
> *1 Peter 1:18, 19*

In John, chapter one, Jesus Christ is repeatedly called *The Lamb of God.*

Shout Of Victory

The final words from the cross are revealing. As He gave up His spirit, Jesus cried out, *"It is finished!"* The actual words He used mean *paid in full.* At that time, when a debt had been legally discharged, authorities would stamp papers containing charges against an individual with this phrase indicating the debt had been paid in full.

This was the cry of victory. The battle was over. The debt for sin had been paid in full. What Jesus Christ had set out to do was completed, and God the Father was fully satisfied forever. Never again would man need to shed blood in order to come into the presence of a Holy God.

This was God's plan, love's highest hour.

Left on our own, every one of us is destined to receive God's wrath, which is the just response of a Holy God toward sin. But God has devised a way to spare us that wrath. In His mercy and love for man, there can be forgiveness for every one of our failures because His Son died in our place. He took the wrath we would have incurred upon Himself.

More Than A Pardon

What God our Father did through Jesus His Son on Calvary is more than a pardon for those who desire it. It is *exoneration*. It is being declared innocent as if the lies we have told have never been said and our moments of failure have never occurred. The book of Romans reveals this justification:

> *Being justified as a gift by His grace through the redemption which is in Christ Jesus; whom God displayed publicly as a propitiation by His blood through faith. This was to demonstrate His righteousness, because in His forbearance God had passed over the sins previously committed to demonstrate, at the present time His righteousness, that He might be just and the justifier of the one who has faith in Jesus.*
>
> *Romans 3:24-26*

Justification comes from God. Someone has said about justification, *"It is just-as-if-I'd-never-sinned."* This is true. Righteousness in the eyes of God can be ours. It is an exchanged life, the righteousness of Jesus Christ in exchange for my sin-filled life.

The Veil Of The Temple Torn

As Jesus breathed His last, the 20-foot-high, 60-foot-long curtain covering the Holy of Holies in the temple was split supernaturally from top to bottom. Woven of dense linen fiber as thick as a man's palm, this massive curtain had served as a barrier, separating man from God's presence for centuries. It was now taken down by God Himself, revealing to all the world that His presence was open to those who would come to Him through faith in the finished work of Jesus Christ. The book of Hebrews tells us:

> *Since therefore, brethren, we have confidence*
> *to enter the holy place by the blood of Jesus, by*
> *a new and living way which He inaugurated*
> *for us through the veil that is, His flesh ...*
> *Hebrews 10:19, 20*

Reconciliation between God and all mankind became possible that day on the cross. The door is open into God's presence for any individual who will enter. A decision is set before every man.

The Door

Jesus Christ is the door to God the Father. He is the door each person walks through to enter into eternal life. In the book of John, Jesus is quoted as saying:

> *I am the door; if anyone enters through Me,*
> *he shall be saved ...*
>
> *John 10:9*

This eternal relationship with God the Father, through Jesus the Son, is God's gift for anyone who will come. Entering into this relationship is a personal decision. If you enter in, God has known you would do so. From the foundation of the earth, He has known you would come.

Unopened Gift

To countless people in every generation, this life-changing relationship remains an unopened gift, one offered yet never received. God's gift is mine. It is yours.

It has been purchased for us at an unbelievably high price, but it is a gift waiting to be opened. If we desire it, we must personally reach out for this gift and take it for our own.

Receiving God's gift comes through faith in the finished work of Jesus Christ. The moment of embracing His gift marks the moment of adoption into God's family. The New Testament declares:

> *But as many as received Him (Jesus Christ), to them He gave the right to become children of God, to those who believe in His name, who were born not of blood, nor of the will of the flesh, but of God.*
>
> *John 1:12, 13*

Reading this verse, we see that this is a *birth* that God Himself brings to pass within a person who receives Christ by faith. This is the *second birth.* "Born again," a phrase which has received considerable publicity in recent years, was first used by Jesus Himself when He said:

> *Do not marvel that I said to you, "You must be born again."*
>
> *John 3:7*

Jesus is speaking of the spiritual rebirth needed to come into God's presence. Our first birth is physical, by an act of our parents, but this verse is speaking of something entirely different. This birth is something God brings about within us as our *spirit*, rather than our body, comes to life. Jesus said:

> *Truly, truly, I say to you, unless one is born of water and the Spirit, he cannot enter into*

the kingdom of God. That which is born of
the flesh is flesh, and that which is born of
the Spirit is spirit.

John 3:5, 6

There Is No Formula

In receiving the gift of eternal life, a person becomes spiritually alive, born into God's eternal family. This experience cannot be put into a formula, because God brings it about in a million different ways. By growing up in a family of faith and being taught from infancy truths concerning Jesus Christ, one may never be able to pinpoint that certain time of placing faith in Jesus Christ.

Some may come to faith in Christ through a sermon, others through a television program, while others come through a book, a tract, a conversation, or reading Scripture on their own, but in every case, it is the Holy Spirit revealing truth to the individual involved. God is all creative in capturing a person's heart.

Head Knowledge Versus Heart Knowledge

Many individuals have head knowledge instead of heart knowledge. Theological facts are of critical importance, but good theology will always involve the person's intellect kindled with an emotional response of the heart.

People today may know numerous facts about Jesus Christ. They have heard that Jesus was crucified on a cross and died for sin. But those facts have been filed away, never to touch their hearts or affect their lives in any way. Some have attended church for years and even taught Sunday School, but they have never been put in touch with God the Father, through Jesus the Son, which makes all the difference in the world.

Knowing God

The difference is *knowing God.* This relationship, once forged, does far more than monitor externals; the human heart is fully engaged. This encounter is personal. It is one-on-one with the Creator. It is life-changing.

Relationship Not Religion

Christ brings us into a relationship, not a religion. You will know the difference when it becomes a reality in your life. Jesus Christ makes the difference. He is the way to the Father. Jesus said:

> *I am the way, the truth, and the life; no one comes to the Father but through Me.*
> *John 14:6*

There is a step to take. We have been given the way, but we must go through the door. While there is every reason for a person to take the step of faith toward God, many will not. Most people profess belief in the reality of God, but many find excuses not to become personally involved with Him or to commit their lives to Him.

Unworthy

Some people hesitate because they feel they are unworthy and must clean up their life before they can approach God. But no one, on his own, has the power it takes to make lasting change. It is God's Spirit within a person that will make the difference. Jesus said He came to seek and to save the lost and the sinful, not the righteous. No matter where you are in life, what addictions you have, or what you have done, God loves you and is waiting for you to come to Him just as you are. His transforming power will help make any necessary changes after you belong to Him.

What About Those Who Never Hear?

Some refuse the invitation Jesus offers because they know there are many in the world who will never hear the Gospel of Jesus Christ, and they feel it is not fair that some hear while others never have the opportunity. But the Bible reveals that within every person is an innate awareness that God exists. It is implanted within man. Scripture clearly states this in the book of Romans:

> *For the wrath of God is revealed from heaven against all ungodliness and unrighteousness of men, who suppress the truth in unrighteousness, because that which is known about God is evident within them; for God made it evident to them. For since the creation of the world His invisible attributes, His eternal power, and divine nature, have been clearly seen, being understood through what has been made so that they are without excuse.*
>
> *Romans 1:18-20*

God has given to every individual revelation concerning Himself, and He sees the response a person has to that revelation. His Word says every seeking heart will find Him. He sees what man cannot, the thoughts and intentions of every heart. God is perfect justice, and

Scripture tells us His ways are higher than our ways and beyond man's understanding in this life.

What About The Hypocrites?

Others do not come to Christ because they cannot get past the hypocrites in Church. But Jesus taught that hypocrites would always be in the midst of His Church. He said the good wheat (believers) would grow up right beside weeds (unbelievers). No one should weed them out because, in doing so, younger future believers may also leave (like children who attend with a father who is a hypocrite). We are not to concern ourselves about this matter because one day Jesus Himself will separate the good wheat from the chaff. That day is coming. The problem is not hypocrites. The problem is our own personal response.

Some Feel Sin Is Not An Issue In Their Life

There are individuals who feel they do not need Jesus Christ because sin is not an issue in their life. They truly attempt to live an exemplary life and therefore, they do not need help, but Scripture reveals every man has sinned and is in need of a Savior. Sin is sin in God's eyes. Gossip, pride, or judgmental thoughts separate a person from God just as much as another man's murder or incest does. All have missed the mark of God's perfection. The Bible clearly teaches:

> *... all have sinned and fall short of the glory of God.*
>
> *Romans 3:23*

We have all sinned and Scripture tells us:

For the wages of sin is death (separation from God) but the free gift of God is eternal life in Jesus Christ our Lord.

Romans 6:23

God's Gift Is Free

People work all their lives for the wages of sin which is death, but the gift of eternal life is not available for wages. It is free. People try to work their way to Heaven, but they will never make it, no matter how good they are. God says there is one way to come into His presence and that is by faith.

Step Of Faith Required

God requires every person to take a step of faith in order to receive His gift of eternal life. Faith is not a feeling. It is an inner conviction and belief in that which we cannot see. We come on God's terms or not at all. He says all come to Him through faith. The book of Hebrews tells us:

But without faith it is impossible to please Him (God), for he who comes to God must believe that He is, and that He is a rewarder of those who diligently seek Him.

Hebrews 11:6

Although faith does not hinge on feelings, if you feel you lack faith, ask God to help you with your unbelief. He is more than willing to help those who are seeking Him. The Bible tells us even our faith is a gift from God.

We are told:

> *For by grace you have been saved through*
> *faith: and that not of yourself, it is the gift of*
> *God; not as a result of works, that no one*
> *should boast.*
>
> *Ephesians 2:8, 9*

We All Enter God's Presence The Same Way

Those of rags and those of riches all enter into God's presence the same way. It does not matter if one is Presbyterian, Methodist, Catholic, Baptist, Lutheran, Pentecostal, or has never darkened the door of a church. It does not matter if we have several degrees behind our name or if we have never had any formal education. Each one of us is asked to step out in faith and place our trust in Christ's finished work on the cross in order to enter into God's eternal presence.

By taking this step of faith, then revelation comes. Man says, *"Seeing is believing,"* but God says, *"Believe and you will see."*

Come and Dine

God invites you to take your own step of faith and open His gift. Jesus extends to you the following invitation:

> *Behold I stand at the door and knock; if any man hears My voice and opens the door I will come in and dine with him, and he with Me.*
>
> *Revelation 3:20*

Dine With Him

When this invitation was offered, the dining experience was an intimate occasion. Friends and family reclined and relaxed together, dipping from the same bowl. Jesus has said we will have that kind of close relationship with Him when we take a step of faith and open the door. He is the perfect gentleman and never forces open the door to a heart. He issues the invitation and awaits our response.

If you desire to open the gift of eternal life that God is offering to you, it can become yours right now by praying a simple prayer. You may pray aloud or silently. It does not matter. God is always listening and He knows your heart. His Spirit is there with you now. You may talk to Him as you would to a close friend. The important thing is to think about what you are saying and to say it from your heart.

A Simple Prayer

You may receive Christ as your Savior in any words you wish to use, but if you would like help, the following prayer is sufficient:

God, I confess that I am a sinner, and I understand that I need a Savior. I believe You gave your Son to die in my place, and through His blood, my sins are forgiven. Right now, I want to receive the gift of eternal life and begin a relationship with You.

Jesus, I ask You to come into my life and be my Lord. I thank You that, even as I speak these words, You are entering into my life, and You promise You will never leave me. Please lead me and guide me from this day forward.

In Jesus' name I pray. Amen.

If you prayed this prayer or something similar in your own words, and meant what you said, Jesus Christ is no longer on the outside desiring to come in, He is now within you. You may not feel any differently than you did before you prayed, but an eternal transaction has taken place. God, in the form of the Holy Spirit, has come in to reside forever within you. God does not lie. His word is true. He said if you ask Him to come into your life, He will come in, and if you sincerely asked Him to come in, He did.

Well-meaning individuals, throughout their lives, repeatedly ask Jesus Christ to come into their lives, but this is not necessary. Asking Jesus to come into one's life is a one time process that need never be repeated. He has already come in, and He promises He will never leave you or forsake you.

Born Of The Spirit

You have been born again of the Spirit. Your spirit, that part of every man that is eternal, has come to life and is now able to have fellowship with God the Father. You have become now part of the body of Christ. True believers are called the body of Christ on earth for we are His mouth, hands and feet as we speak out for Him and go out in service for Him.

Within your life a new and wonderful power, the Holy Spirit, now resides. You will become aware that He is with you. Scripture states that God's Spirit will bear witness with your spirit that you have become His. It will be one of the most thrilling things in life as you begin to experience His presence.

To understand the Holy Spirit and the incredible power that is now yours, we must return to the cross and the tomb where Jesus Christ was laid.

PART II

Futile Precautions

Observing the final breaths of Jesus Christ, the Roman soldiers bypassed the routine procedure of breaking His legs to hasten death. Instead, they pierced His side with a spear. Blood and water came forth, irrefutable evidence that death had occurred. Unknowingly, these men fulfilled two prophecies concerning the Messiah declared hundreds of years before that not a bone of His body would be broken (*Psalm 34:20*) and that He would be pierced (*Psalm 22:16*).

A prominent member of the Jewish Council, Joseph of Arimathea, who secretly had been a disciple of Christ, courageously came forward to request that the body of Jesus be released to him for burial. Pilate honored his request. Because sundown was near and the Sabbath was approaching, the body was hastily anointed with spices, wrapped in strips of white linen, and laid in Joseph of Arimathea's own tomb, fulfilling yet another prophecy that the Messiah was to be buried in the grave of the rich (*Isaiah 53:9*).

They Were Uneasy

One might assume that the Jews who had accomplished this crucifixion would be celebrating the demise of their enemy, but they continued to fear the influence of Jesus Christ. They remembered Jesus had said He would rise again after three days. Concerned that His disciples would try to steal the body, they insisted that stringent precautions be taken to guard His tomb. They approached the Roman authorities and Pontius Pilate, saying:

> *Sir, we remember that when He was still alive that deceiver said, "After three days I am to rise again." Therefore give orders for the grave to be made secure until the third day, lest the disciples come and steal Him away and say to the people, "He has risen from the dead," and the last deception will be worst than the first.*
> *Matthew 27:63, 64*

The Romans accommodated. A large stone was rolled in front of the tomb, which was shut with the Roman seal. Breaking that seal carried the death penalty. Roman guards were stationed at the site around the clock.

The Grave Could Not Hold Him

These were futile precautions in light of what was about to happen. Hundreds of Roman soldiers could not stop this grave from opening. According to the gospels, Jesus Christ had ruined every funeral He had attended by restoring life to the lifeless. He had said that He would be raised on the third day, and He was!

Jesus rose through those linen wrappings and those cave walls as if they were not there. Left behind was a cocoon of bandages and guards who, Scripture records, lay like dead men from fright as the Roman seal burst open and the huge stone was rolled away by an angel of the Lord. The stone was rolled away, not so that Jesus could get out of the tomb, but so that man could get in and see that Jesus Christ was no longer there.

Although Jesus had told His disciples many times of His coming death and resurrection, nothing prepared them for the empty tomb. No one expected this. Neither the Roman soldiers, the women who loved Him, nor any of His disciples expected Jesus to rise from the dead. The Jewish religious authorities did not expect this. They suspected grave robbers, not resurrection.

Convincing His Disciples

With a body that now went through walls and locked doors, that very day, Jesus began to appear to His disciples, who had scattered in disillusionment and fear following the crucifixion. Even in a room behind closed doors, suddenly there He would be, in their midst. One of the disciples, Thomas, when told of the resurrection of Jesus Christ, doubted the other disciples' eyewitness accounts saying that unless he could personally put his own finger into the nailprints in the hand of Jesus and touch His side where it had been pierced, he would never believe. Eight days later, Jesus appeared to the disciples and said to Thomas:

> *Reach your finger, and see My hands; and*
> *reach here your hand, and put it into My*
> *side; and be not unbelieving, but believing.*
> *John 20:27*

Thomas believed. Over the next forty days, He was seen time and time again by those who loved Him. No longer did Jesus Christ appear to those whose hearts were closed toward Him.

Jesus was seen by over five hundred of His followers on one occasion. He cooked for His disciples. He ate with them. Jesus Christ did whatever it took to convince those who loved Him that He was resurrected from the dead and very much alive. Jesus had a job for His followers to carry out in the future, and to do it they would have to believe they had a risen Savior.

A Message For Mankind

There was a message His disciples were to deliver to mankind. It was a message Jesus had spent three years preparing this small band of men to declare to the world. This message today is termed "the Gospel." The Gospel means "good news," and the good news Jesus Christ wanted them to share was the fact that:

> *God so loved the world, that He gave His*
> *only begotten Son, that whoever believes in*
> *Him should not perish, but have eternal life.*
> *John 3:16*

Jesus wanted the world to know that eternal life and forgiveness of sins are available to anyone who will believe in Him. This was the message they were to deliver. The work of Christ on earth was to continue. In fact, it was just getting started.

Final Instructions

When the disciples were fully convinced He was alive and not dead, Jesus left them, ascending into Heaven before their very eyes. They would see Him no more in this life. But before leaving, Jesus gave these men final instructions. He made it clear to His disciples they were *not* to attempt this work at that time. They were to stay in Jerusalem and *wait*. These were strange instructions. The disciples must have wondered what Jesus meant as He told them:

> ... *behold, I am sending forth the promise of My Father upon you, but you are to stay in the city until you are clothed with power from on high.*
>
> Luke 24:49

Clothed with *"power from on high"*? What kind of power? What did this mean?

The Power

Returning to Jerusalem, this faithful band of men and women were obedient to the instructions they had been given. They waited in the city. Ten days later, on the day of Pentecost, that *"power from on high"* arrived. Roaring into Jerusalem with a sound like a tremendous hurricane, it brought people running from all over the city to see what was happening. It was the Holy Spirit coming down and entering into those who believed in Jesus Christ.

The Helper

Jesus had told His followers that it would be to their advantage if He went away. They had heard Him say:

> *But I tell you the truth, it is to your advantage that I go away; for if I do not go away, the Helper shall not come to you; but if I go, I will send Him to you.*
>
> *John 16:7*

The Holy Spirit was the Helper sent by God to come down and dwell within them and to clothe them with power from on high. This was the Spirit of truth whom Jesus referred to when He had said:

> *...I will ask the Father, and He will give you another helper that He may be with you forever; that is the Spirit of truth, whom the world cannot receive, because it does not behold him or know Him, but you know Him because He abides with you, and will be in you.*
>
> *John 14:16, 17*

The Holy Spirit had been with them, but now He entered into each one of them. Jesus knew it was humanly impossible for these men and women to carry out the job He had given them to do in their own strength. God was getting ready to do a new work through men and women which would require supernatural ability, and the power to carry it out had just arrived. The Holy Spirit would be their strength and help for what lay ahead. They would need it. Many of them were destined to die a martyr's death in the days to come.

Supernatural Ability

As the Holy Spirit entered into them, these disciples, who had been hiding in fear for their lives, hit the streets. They not only began to speak out publicly, but they were given supernatural ability to speak languages they had never known. People from all over the world, visiting Jerusalem for the Feast of Pentecost, were able to hear in their own native language the message that Jesus Christ wanted them to hear. All of this was done through the power of the Holy Spirit.

Three Thousand Came To Christ That Day

Empowered by the Spirit, Peter, the disciple who only days before had fearfully denied that he knew Jesus Christ, now stood boldly proclaiming God's message about salvation through Jesus Christ. Three thousand were brought to a saving knowledge of Christ that very day, and as they individually believed in their hearts that Jesus Christ had died for them, the Holy Spirit also entered into them.

Many of these new believers would return to their own countries to proclaim this message now burning within their hearts. The Church was in motion, and the world would never be the same.

The Tables Turned

We can assume the Jewish religious leaders who had gotten rid of Jesus Christ were standing on the fringes of the crowd not believing their eyes. How could an illiterate fisherman like Peter speak with such authority? These enemies of Christ must have been visibly sick as they heard the impossible come forth from very ordinary men.

Thousands In His Place

They did not understand that what is impossible with man is possible through the transforming power of the Holy Spirit. If these powerful men thought they had problems with Jesus Christ traveling about teaching, how in the world would they handle over three thousand people, empowered by the Holy Spirit, speaking out about eternal life through Jesus Christ? They had killed One, only to discover they now had thousands in His place. Their problems were just beginning.

Many of these irate men would spend the rest of their lives trying to eradicate a movement which would come to be known as "The Way," referring to the way that one receives salvation. They would never succeed because their opponent was God Himself. Their persecution would only fan the fires of this movement. Those once-cowering disciples were destined to turn the world upside down.

Millions Would Die

Early church history records that all but one of the eleven remaining disciples would die a violent death for the cause of Christ, but hundreds would take their place. Millions were to die over the centuries. Ripped apart by wild animals as entertainment for decadent spectators and lit up as human torches for Nero's garden parties, they died for the privilege of adding others to God's kingdom and the right to declare that which was unshakable within them, that Jesus Christ is Lord. They chose death rather than renouncing their faith.

The Holy Spirit Within

From the day of Pentecost forward, God, in the form of the Holy Spirit, has taken up residence within every person who will take that step of faith, placing trust in the saving work of Jesus Christ. He is doing it today. This message still goes out, and lives are still being radically changed.

You Too Are Empowered

If you have prayed to receive Christ, placing your trust in the fact that He died in your place, you too are empowered to share the Gospel with others who need to hear this message. There is a new power in your life. It is the Holy Spirit. In time, if you desire it, the Holy Spirit will not only equip you and bring opportunities of service your way, but He will give you the words to say and the courage to say them. Through the power of the Holy Spirit, your life will begin to be used to enlarge and enhance the kingdom of Jesus Christ, and then one day you will be rewarded for making yourself available. Whatever you give to Jesus Christ, He will return to you many times over.

His Spirit Within

Called "the Comforter," the Holy Spirit, according to Scripture, will become that friend who sticks closer than a brother. The Holy Spirit will go before you and open doors you could never open on your own. He will close doors with your welfare in mind. He will answer prayers in creative ways that are above and beyond what you have asked and will be your strength in life's toughest times. The closer you walk with Him, the more real He will become to you.

New Leadership

For years you have been at the helm of your life, but now, if the Spirit has come in, you have an opportunity to be under brand new leadership. It perhaps has been easy to fudge on an expense account or lie in situations before, but the Holy Spirit's convicting power will now disturb your conscience, and it will no longer be a simple issue. The Holy Spirit will not force His hand in your life, but if you allow Him to have His way, He will lead and guide you toward God's perfect will for your life.

Victory Over Habitual Sin

It is the power of the Holy Spirit which enables us to conquer habitual sin. Before the Spirit comes into our lives, we do not have the power to bring about lasting change, but His Spirit will convict and enable us to overcome things which have pulled us down in the past. Becoming a Christian does not mean we no longer sin, but it does mean that, through Christ, we have power over habitual sin. As we grow spiritually, we will begin to have a strong desire to control such things as gossip, lust, lying, substance abuse, compromise in monetary matters, or any other problem area in our life.

Confession

The Holy Spirit is a person. Scripture tells us He can be grieved. He does not leave us when we sin, but our relationship with Him is affected until we confess and forsake things we have said or done outside of His will. Scripture tells us:

> *If we confess our sins, He is faithful and righteous to forgive us our sins and to cleanse us from all unrighteousness.*
>
> *1 John 1:9*

Read this verse carefully. We are to name our sins to God. It is not that He does not know our every thought and action, but He wants us to deal with Him personally about our problems and acknowledge that we cannot handle them on our own. According to this verse, if we will confess the sins we know of, He will not only cleanse us from those sins, but He will then also cleanse us from the ones of which we are unaware.

Mental Health

What a fantastic promise! We cannot possibly be conscious of all the wrongs we commit on a regular basis whether it be a prideful attitude, judgmental thoughts, or lack of consideration for another, but God forgives all our sins when we confess the obvious ones. Being *forgiven* is an integral factor in mental health. Hospitals and counseling centers today are overflowing with people who cannot get rid of their guilt. Only through Christ does true forgiveness and peace of mind come into one's life.

Repentance

Sincere confession of sin will always involve repentance. Repentance means turning around and walking in the opposite direction of the sin we have confessed. Conquering sin requires a decision on our part to participate in that offense no longer. Scripture promises us that:

> *No temptation has overtaken you but such as is common to man; and God is faithful, Who will not allow you to be tempted beyond what you are able, but with the temptation will provide the way of escape also, that you may be able to endure it.*
>
> *1 Corinthians 10:13*

The way of escape is there. This is a promise of God. There will always be a way out of sin, yet it will require an act of our will to take God's escape in tempting situations.

Real change will take time. A liar is still a liar, in his heart and by habit, when he decides that he will no longer lie, but as he acts on that conviction by refusing to lie, in time, God changes his very nature and he no longer is a liar.

Some of us have real mountains to climb. Occasionally God will deliver a believer from alcoholism or drug addiction or some other overwhelming bondage overnight, but this is not the norm. If God chooses to do that, it is perhaps because He knows there are many other problems in a particular life to overcome and, in His mercy, He will get that one big obstacle out of the way. However, in the usual pattern of Christian life, God builds patience and character into our lives as He helps us overcome problems, trials, and temptations. God knows that through the power of the Holy Spirit, we have what it takes to conquer those seemingly immovable mountains. It will take time, but He is an infinitely patient and loving Father who helps us every step of the way.

He Accepts You Just As You Are

Despite any habit, addiction, attitude, or circumstance you may face, God loves you. He cannot love you any more than he does right now. He is in the business of changing lives, but your heavenly Father accepts you and loves you with His perfect love just as you are right now.

If your earthly father has been a loving, personal, supportive father to you, then it should not be difficult for you to receive the intimate love and support God the Father has for you through His Spirit. If, however, your earthly father has been harsh, non-communicative, abusive, or absent, then it may be far more difficult for you to perceive God the Father as He really is. Again, it will take time, but God knows every hurt you have ever experienced, and He also knows the healing process He will use in your life to make you whole.

Build Upon
Your Foundation

In receiving Christ, you have laid a foundation for eternity. Scripture tells us:

> *For no man can lay a foundation other than*
> *the one which is laid, which is Jesus Christ.*
> *1 Corinthians 3:11*

Laying this foundation is the single most important thing you will ever do, but it is the bare beginning in a lifelong process. You will build upon this foundation. It is the building process from this point forward that will tell the story of your life in the end. Scripture tells us to add to our foundation with that which has lasting and eternal value.

How does one build on the foundation that has been laid by receiving Christ? Several crucial avenues exist to bring one to maturity, and God has given us specific instructions regarding each of these areas. God carefully prepares and equips, with knowledge and practical experience, those who will allow Him to mold them into vessels fit for use in His kingdom's work.

Prayer

Prayer, one of the greatest powers available in the universe, is a beginning step. As you talk to God, know that He is there with you and within you. The focus of prayer is God Himself, fellowship, and friendship with Him. He is delighted when you speak to Him. He wants our wildest joys and excitement shared with Him. He also tells us to:

> *"Be still and know that I am God."*
> *Psalm 46:10*

The Hebrew word translated *be still* literally means "let go of your grip." God wants us to let go of our greatest concerns, fear, anger, and disappointments by bringing them to Him and trusting Him to help us deal with them. He is more than able to handle whatever we bring to Him. He knows all things already, but He loves for us to be honest with our feelings before Him and involve Him in the hard things we go through.

Do not be discouraged if prayer is difficult at first. A thousand distractions may come. Your mind will wander, you will think of things you need to do, or phones will ring. Pause, write those things down, and continue. Persevere. God rewards those who will pay the price to come close to Him. It will be during prayer that you will receive creative ideas, visions for ministry, or solutions to problems which would never have occurred to you on your own. They will come to you from the Holy Spirit.

Prayer will change your life because God hears and He never forgets. He is the God who answers above and beyond what we ask, and we never know what He is going to do. Our answers may seem long in coming from our perspective or not at all what we had our hopes set on, but He who sees and knows all is at work for our good. One of the greatest privileges we have on earth is that we may come into His presence at any time.

Bible Study

Beginning to study God's word is another invaluable building block in adding to your foundation. Every word of Scripture is divinely inspired, and it will do things in your life that nothing else can. Scripture reveals that when God's word goes out it accomplishes that which he has sent it forth to do. The Bible is the supernatural instrument and vehicle God has left on earth to edify, change, and equip us.

Precepts and principles will be engrafted into your life as time is spent in His word. Old thought patterns are torn down, changing the way you react to circumstances, as you begin to view life from an eternal perspective. A peace and security, not of this world, will begin to take hold in your life.

Before the Holy Spirit came into your life, you could not understand God's Word because it is understood only through the Holy Spirit. Speaking of the Spirit, Scripture reveals:

> *But a natural man does not accept the things of the Spirit of God; for they are foolishness to him, and he cannot understand them, because they are spiritually appraised.*
>
> *1 Corinthians 2:14*

If you have tried to read the Bible before receiving Christ, it perhaps seemed difficult or put you to sleep. Now, His Spirit within will open up His word and help you understand. Having God personally speak to you through His Word will be one of the most exciting things you have ever experienced.

Begin With A Gospel

A good place to begin in the Bible is the New Testament with one of the gospels: Matthew, Mark, Luke, or John. There are many excellent Bible studies that can be purchased at a Christian bookstore in which you will be able to think through and answer questions over a portion of Scripture. As you do this, insights will open up to you as you begin to grasp in a tangible, hands-on way how His commandments, character qualities, and life principles can be lived out in everyday life. Jesus is recorded in the book of John saying:

> *He who has My commandments and keeps them, he it is who loves Me; and he who loves Me shall be loved by My Father, and I will love him, and will disclose Myself to him.*
> *John 14:21*

One way God measures our love for Him is by the effort we make to learn and keep His commandments. Apart from being in His word, we will never learn them. When we do, God begins to reveal Himself to us in ways beyond our imagination. God delights and surprises those who spend time in His word.

God considers Scripture of such importance that the Bible says heaven and earth will pass away, but His word is forever. Scripture call God's word *a lamp for our feet and a light to our path.*

Fellowship

Building upon a foundation will include finding a church where you will grow to feel at home and where God's Word is taught. You may have to visit several churches before you find the right one for you, but to grow, it is helpful to have fellowship with other Christians and the guidance of a pastor, a priest, or other mature believers. Ask God to lead you to the fellowship He has for you.

Beginning a prayer life, entering into Bible study, establishing relationships with other Christians, and becoming a part of a Bible teaching church, will enable you to build upon your foundation. These are critical for growth and for discovering God's special plan for your life.

Foreordained Works

As you take these steps, each one serves a purpose. This is His equipping. God is preparing you for that which He has called you to do. He has special work which He designed, with you in mind, to be carried out to build up His kingdom on earth. Scripture reveals that:

> *We are His workmanship, **created** in Christ Jesus for **good works which God prepared beforehand**, that we should walk in them.*
> *Ephesians 2:10*

God has created good works just for you. You will always have the choice whether or not you will do those good works, but He has planned specific jobs for you as His child to do. He will equip you to do this work through the necessary talent, training, and knowledge of His word, and then one day, He will reward you for carrying out on earth.

You may miss the opportunity to do what God intends to do through you if you do not grow and go on to maturity in Christ or simply choose not to do what He convicts you to do. God's work will still be accomplished, but someone else will get the blessing for doing it and the reward in eternity.

Christian maturity produces people who are able to respond with love in difficult situations. It does not matter if you are head of a large corporate office, on a nursing staff, an educator, a homemaker, or in full time ministry. All of these jobs will be carried out much more smoothly by one who has grown with His Lord to the point that he or she operates in a Christ-like fashion and can be an effective witness for the kingdom.

It Is Not Too Late

Perhaps you feel you do not have a lot of time to grow in Christ because most of your life has been spent, and it seems futile to attempt to serve God at this late date. Nothing could be further from the truth. Even if you are confined to bed, your prayers can accomplish more for the kingdom than you will ever know.

A parable in the Book of Luke reveals that those who come into His kingdom late in life and serve Him well may receive the same reward as someone who has known Christ since he was young and has labored for Him for years. In our minds this may seem unfair, but again God's ways are not our ways.

He is perfect justice. God has known exactly when you would come into His family, the time you have left, the opportunities you will have, the desire of your heart to serve Him, and the action that you will take to carry out that desire.

Accepting Christ Does Not Eliminate Problems

If you have accepted Christ, your real life is just beginning. It will not be easy. Never let anyone tell you that becoming a Christian will eliminate problems. This is not true. Some people teach or preach that Christians should enjoy health, wealth, and happiness, but reality and Scripture teach just the opposite. Scripture reveals that in this world true followers of Jesus Christ will encounter trials and trouble, but even in the pain and trials we experience, God is at work and He will use them for good in our lives. One of the great promises in Scripture is:

> *And we know that God causes all things to work together for good to those who love God, to those who are called according to His purpose.*
> *Romans 8:28*

We will experience His hand of faithfulness in our toughest and darkest times. Our trust and our joy is in the Lord and not in our circumstances. As our faith matures, we grow to have peace beyond explanation, for we know that God is well aware of our circumstances. He has allowed them and He will use them for our good.

You now have direct and unrestricted access to God's throne. You will experience help from on high to get you through whatever life brings your way. Above all, you will know that He is with you.

The Judgment Seat of Christ

One day we will appear before the judgment seat of Christ. The Bible states:

> For we must all appear before the judgment seat of Christ, that each one may be recompensed for his deeds in the body, according to what he has done, whether good or bad.
>
> *2 Corinthians 5:10*

Only believers, those who have received Christ, will appear before this judgment seat. Those who have not received Christ during their lifetime will not be there. The Bible reveals that they are to be judged at a different place and time. As a child of God, you will stand in this place of judgment. It is a judgment seat. Will you be judged for your sins?

No. Your sins were judged two thousand years ago when Jesus shed His blood on Calvary. From the moment you receive Christ, God no longer sees your sin, not because your life is without sin, but because He sees you washed clean, white as snow, by the blood of the sacrificial lamb He provided, Jesus Christ. Although you still sin and need to confess those sins, God sees from the beginning to the end. He sees you as you will be one day, perfect because you have received His Son. He remembers your sin no more. In Hebrews, we are assured:

> *And their sins and their lawless deeds I will remember no more.*
>
> *Hebrews 10:17*

So, it is not for sin that you will be judged at this judgment seat because your sin in God's eyes is already gone.

What You Did For Christ

Scripture indicates this judgment seat is solely to reveal what one has done for Jesus Christ from the moment he or she comes to know Him. A record of our life is kept by God after we receive His spirit. He sees what we do and the motives behind our actions. Scripture tells us even our prayers are saved and recorded in heaven. Whatever we have done for Christ will be an open book that day.

Human nature is such that even believers at times make the right moves for the wrong reasons. Sometimes our Christian works are done out of habit, for the praise of men or for our own personal advancement rather than for love of God and our fellow man. There will be those at the judgment seat of Christ whose works will have all been worthless. About that day, we are told in Scripture:

Now if any man builds upon the foundation with gold, silver, precious stones, wood, hay, straw, each man's work will become evident; for the day will show it, because it is to be revealed with fire; and the fire itself will test the quality of each man's work. If any man's work which he has built upon it remains, he shall receive a reward. If any man's work is burned up, he shall suffer loss; but he himself shall be saved, yet so as through fire.

1 Corinthians 3:12-15

Treasure In Heaven

Jesus Christ will have rewards that day for those who have chosen to make their life count for His kingdom and have carried out the works that He has prepared for them to do. Only God would design good works for us so that one day He could reward us for doing them. We cannot imagine what those rewards will be. We are told in the New Testament:

Things which eye has not seen and ear has not heard, and which have not entered the heart of man, all that God has prepared for those who love Him.

1 Corinthians 2:9

The rewards received will still bring us pleasure ten million years from now and beyond. That is why Jesus says:

Do not lay up for yourselves treasures upon earth, where moth and rust destroy, and

> *where thieves break in and steal. But lay up*
> *for yourselves treasures in heaven, where*
> *neither moth nor rust destroys, and where*
> *thieves do not break in or steal; for where*
> *your treasure is, there will your heart be also.*
> *Matthew 6:19, 20, 21*

Though we can take nothing with us when we leave this earth, we can send it ahead.

God compares this life to a blade of grass, here one day and gone tomorrow. It is but one second compared to the millions of years we will spend in eternity. Yet it is this life, what we have done in the here and now, that will determine what eternity will be like for us individually. There is no reincarnation or second chance as some would have you believe. Scripture clearly states that:

> *... it is appointed for men to die once*
> *and after this comes judgment.*
> *Hebrews 9:27*

The fact that this life is like our final exam is part of God's plan. When we come to Christ, it is like God hands to each one of us the script of the rest of our life and says, *"Here, you finish it anyway you want to."* If we have received God's gift of eternal life, our script is being written. One day all of our opportunities will be over, and not one of us knows when that time will come. God wants to reward, for all eternity, those who make the decision to live for Him rather than for what this world has to offer. Someone has said and it is true:

> *"Only one life ... it will soon be past.*
> *Only what is done for Christ will last."*

Messianic Prophecies

Old Testament Prophecy	New Testament Fulfillment

He would be born in Bethlehem

Micah 5:2	Matthew 2:1
	Luke 2:4-6

His mother would be a Jewish virgin

Isaiah 7:14	Matthew 1:18-25

The Messiah would be called out of Egypt

Hosea 11:1	Matthew 2:15

He would be of the tribe of Judah

Genesis 49:10	Matthew 1:2
	Luke 3:33

He would be of the seed of Abraham

Genesis 12:3, 18:18	Luke 3:34

King David would be His ancestor

Psalm 132:11, Isaiah 11:10	Matthew 1:6
Jeremiah 23:5, 33:15	Luke 1:32-33

He would heal the lame, deaf, dumb, blind

Isaiah 35:5, 6	John 11:47
	Matthew 11:3-6

He would minister to the Gentiles
Isaiah 42:1, 49:1-8   Matthew 12:21

The Messiah would be betrayed by a friend
Psalm 41:9   John 13:18, 21

He would be betrayed for 30 pieces of silver
Zechariah 11:12   Matthew 26:15

The 30 pieces of silver would buy a potter's field
Zechariah 11:13   Matthew 27:3-10

He would be disfigured by cruelty
Isaiah 52:14   Matthew 27:27-30

He would be beaten and spat upon
Isaiah 50:6   Matthew 27:26, 30

He would be silent before His accusers
Isaiah 53:7   Matthew 27:13, 14

His hands and feet would be pierced
Psalm 22:14-16   John 19:34, 37

He would die by crucifixion
Genesis 12:3, 18:18   John 19:17, 18

They would cast lots for His clothing
Psalm 22:18   Matthew 27:35

He would be forsaken by His disciples
Zechariah 13:7   Matthew 26:31, 36

He would be despised and rejected by men
Isaiah 53:1-3   Mark 15:29-32

He would die as an offering for sin
Isaiah 53:12   2 Corinthians 5:21

He would pray for His enemies
Isaiah 53:12   Luke 23:43

He was the Lamb of God
Isaiah 53:7   John 1:29

He would have a grave with the rich
Isaiah 53:9   Matthew 27:57-60

He was the Shepherd God would smite
Zechariah 13:7   Matthew 26:31

He would be raised from the dead
Psalm 16:10   Matthew 28:1-10
                              Mark 16:1-8

He would ascend into heaven
Zechariah 13:7   Matthew 26:31, 36

He would be at the right hand of God
Psalm 110:1   Hebrews 1:3

Portrait of the Messiah in the Old Testament

Isaiah 53:1-12

1 Who has believed our message? And to whom has the arm of the Lord been revealed?

2 For He grew up before Him like a tender shoot, and like a root out of Parched ground; He has no stately form or majesty that we should look upon Him, nor appearance that we should be attracted to Him.

3 He was despised and forsaken of men, a man of sorrows, and acquainted with grief; and like one from whom men hide their face, He was despised, and we did not esteem Him.

4 Surely our griefs He Himself bore, and our sorrows He carried; Yet we ourselves esteemed Him stricken, smitten of God, and afflicted.

5 But He was pierced through for our transgression, He was crushed for our iniquities; the chastening for our well-being fell upon Him, and by His scourging we are healed.

6 All of us like sheep have gone astray, each of us has turned to his own way; but the Lord has caused the iniquity of us all to fall on Him.

7 He was oppressed and He was afflicted, yet He did not open His mouth; like a lamb that is led to slaughter and like a sheep that is silent before its shearers, so He did not open His mouth.

8 By oppression and judgment He was taken away; and as for His generation, who considered that He was cut off out of the land of the living, for the transgression of my people to whom the stroke was due?

9 His grave was assigned with wicked men, yet He was with a rich man in His death, because He had done no violence, nor was there any deceit in His mouth.

10 But the Lord was pleased to crush Him, putting Him to grief; if He would render Himself as a guilt offering, He will see His offspring, He will prolong His days, and the good pleasure of the Lord will prosper in His hand.

11 As a result of the anguish of His soul, He will see it and be satisfied; by His knowledge the Righteous One, My Servant, will justify the many, As He will bear their iniquities.

12 Therefore, I will allot Him a portion with the great, and He will divide the booty with the strong, because He poured out Himself to death, and was numbered with the transgressors; yet He Himself bore the sin of many, and interceded for the transgressors.

If you would like to share this message with others,
copies of
Open His Gift
may be ordered through:

danataggart@sbcglobal.net

or by calling:

1-361-729-0429